I0464987

How to Work with Difficult People

Understanding Different kinds of Difficult People at Work, at School, in Life and How to Deal with Them

Introduction

I want to thank you and congratulate you for purchasing the book, *"How to Work with Difficult People."*

We all have met and interacted with people we perceived as difficult. It might be at school, at work or even in public spaces. Those people who seem to turn a good day into one of the worst days. It might even be at home. Walking away from these people can be an option but in most cases it's not possible. We simply have to interact with them despite how difficult they are.

People normally complain most about difficult people at school and in workplace. This is normally because you have to work with and interact with these people a lot. Their behavior is more likely to rub you the wrong way. You must work with them to deliver a project or a report. They can be that lazy colleague, that overly demanding boss, rude customers, bullies, aggressive colleagues and henceforth. This list can be very long. Understanding such kind of people and their view of issues will help you in developing strategies to deal with them.

When dealing with difficult people, it's your responsibility to control your part of the interaction to avoid any hostilities. Remember, difficulty is mostly perceived and is not absolute. What you may refer to as difficult behavior might not be so to someone else. We shall be looking more into this later in this book.

In this book, we are going to define difficult people, look at different types of such kind of people, strategies to manage them and how to communicate with them effectively to avoid any unpleasant situations. Lastly we shall look at how to build a resilient mindset to cope with difficult people whenever we encounter them.

Copyright 2015-2016 Ubertec Publishing by Max Smart - All rights reserved

Disclaimer

The information herein is geared towards giving definite and dependable data concerning the theme and issue covered. The distribution is sold with the understanding that the distributor, writer or publisher is not qualified or otherwise to give medical, legal or financial advice. In the event that guidance is needed, a legitimate or proficient person in the profession ought to be sought.

It is unlawful to repeat, copy, or retransmit any piece of this document by either electronic means or in printed configuration. Redistribution of this production in any capacity is not permitted unless the distributor has explicit consent from the author or publisher. All rights held.

The information herein is understood to be truthful. In that any risk, regarding use or misuse, of any approaches, techniques, or direction contained inside is the lone and utter responsibility of the reader. By no means will any legitimate or illegitimate obligation or fault be held against the distributor, publisher, author or other, for any reparation, harms, or money related misfortune because of the data herein, either straightforward or by implication.

Particular creators possess all copyrights not held by the distributor.

The data thus is offered for information purposes only. The presentation of the data is without contract or any kind of insurance certification.

The trademarks that are utilized are without any consent or support by the trademark owner. All trademarks and brands inside this book are for clarifying purposes only and are owned by the owners themselves, not affiliated with this document.

CopyScape Verified June 4, 2015
Edited January 1, 2016

Contents

Chapter 1: Defining Difficult People

CC0 Public Domain pixabay.com

People are not normally difficult; it's their behavior that is difficult. It's not correct to refer to someone as being difficult but we might refer to their personality and behavior as difficult since this is what they have exhibited. When you look more closely at this you'll find that every person is different in terms of personality, upbringing, schooling, beliefs and aspirations. Difficulties therefore arise when people with these different kinds of personalities come together and fail to agree on an issue. Therefore a person can't be labeled difficult per se. However, due to frustrations and anger when we encounter such behaviors we tend to refer to the whole person as difficult. You'll agree with me that there's no particular person who's always difficult, it's in certain circumstances that they appear to be difficult. In other interactions, they might have the best kind of personality to deal with. A difficult colleague at work might have a lovely family and wonderful social life. In fact it's said that we are all somebody's difficult person at some point.

When we have this in mind, we are more likely to understand difficult behavior and explore ways to respond and deal with it. We shouldn't judge too quickly and label a person as difficult to the point that we allow ourselves to be aggrieved and frustrated. We should try to see things from that other person's point of view. However, this doesn't mean we agree or condone their behavior; it's more of a way to gauge our reaction and response. You'll also appreciate their right to have such a view. Working out how best to interact with them will now be the focus rather than trying to change them to fit what we would like of them.

Difficult people might be intimidating, awkward, demanding or in the case of school life even bullish. They can make a situation deteriorate from bad to worse very fast due to their actions and inflexibility. There is a line we should always draw regarding what we can tolerate from them and what we can't. I mentioned bullying and this is something we should never take or tolerate. Sadly enough, bullies are not only found in school but also in the workplace, on our roads and in public areas. Bullies don't just exhibit difficult behavior but might also be overly aggressive, abusive or violent. It's not our responsibility to understand such kind of people. These should be handled by the authorities.

Human interactions over the years have evolved a lot to what it is today. People will use all manner of behaviors and response to achieve an intended outcome. These may either be intentional and well calculated or just out of instinct. For example in the workplace, one person might try to outdo all others by all means disposable to them to gain a promotion. In school, a student might try to get attention by all means. In such instances, they will do anything and in the process might rub shoulders the wrong way thus the perception of difficulty.

Difficult behavior can simply be irritating or far worse, to the extent of jeopardizing relationships and performance at school or at work. Difficult behavior varies widely depending on situations. People can be manipulative jealous, loud, gossipers and much more. All these are traits others might not be comfortable with.

In trying to understanding difficult behavior we should always try to find out if the other person is being difficult on purpose or if it's in their nature to be so. A lot of us have been difficult by being argumentative and obstructive when we didn't want something to happen or had been unhappy about something. For instance in a family situation, a partner might just argue without being objective because they felt aggravated by another unrelated event that happened. This can happen even in the workplace where someone deliberately tries to be difficult to avoid a responsibility. Alternatively, depending on the personality of a person, they may exhibit some difficult characteristics such as being too loud, or too aggressive. They don't mean to hurt you or avoid responsibility, it's just in them. Identifying these two differences will be vital in how to manage such a difficult person.

Difficult people are not just those perceived as aggressive or hostile. In fact other character traits can be more difficult to deal with and lead to a lot of frustrations. For instance, a super agreeable person who over commits and doesn't deliver is difficult to deal with. This brings us to the next chapter where we shall look at the different types of difficult people.

Chapter 2: Types of Difficult People

In both our private and professional lives, we will come across these people. Some might just be a small bother and don't affect our daily life, while others can make us frustrated and angry. These people will seem to be too difficult to deal with, since our personality's clash and nothing seems to get done. However, as you most probably have learnt or will come to learn, we can never escape from difficult people. They are everywhere and the best we can do is to learn how to deal with them. Let's first look at the different types of difficult people.

The bully

CC0 Public Domain pixabay.com

These are normally people with very low self-esteem. They make up for this by harassing others and bringing them down so that they can look good themselves.

This is what normally happens in learning institutions at all levels. The bullies are normally those students who aren't doing well either academically or in co-curricular activities. They thus have a low self-esteem and to boost it up, they tend to harass other students. They want to gain some recognition and attention that they are not getting through their academic efforts. However, and this might come as a surprise to some, bullying is thriving in the workplace as well. Many employees suffer bullying silently. It may not be outright harassment but occurs in some subtle ways such as some false remarks, some backstabbing, some sarcastic comments and so forth. A boss could also be a bully. They may push you with unrealistic targets and shout at you or hurl abuse which can be interpreted as a form of bullying. When dealing with bullies at any levels, do not show them any fear or signs of intimidation. Make it clear to them that you perceive their behaviors as being bullish and are willing to pursue the matter further. Most bullies are cowards and don't like being hit with the truth. They'll thus retract once they realize you are not falling for their bullish behavior.

The jealous type

This is mostly found in the workplace and at school. Someone feels that you are accomplishing more than them and they can't possibly get to your level. They result to using mediocre tactics such as talking ill of you and trying to undermine your achievements. They can be cunning as they can act very supportive and happy for you but the minute you are out of sight, they fall back to their mediocrity. These kind of people are just jealous and probably do not know what they can do to get to your level. The best way to deal with this kind of personality is to approach them and try helping them in their work so that they don't feel inadequate. You should try complementing them in their efforts so that they don't feel as if they are in competition with you. You'll soon realize that when they concentrate on their work and see good results, they stop their jealousy.

The control freaks

These are the kind of people who always have this need to control everybody around them. They want to know what you are doing and everything in between, even when it doesn't concern them at all. They are usually busy trying to micro manage people even when it's not part of their job and thus their productivity will suffer. Usually this behavior is brought about by anxiety. These people are suffering from a constant state of being anxious and thus feel the need to know what other people are doing. They feel they are always right and tend to be "know it all's". They are quick to blame others when something happens to attempt to justify an earlier held position. With these kinds of people, it's advisable to have an honest chat with them and assure them that everything will be ok and they shouldn't overly mind what everybody else is doing. Make them understand that when everybody concentrates on their job, including them, everything will be fine. These people are often insecure and if you confront them with facts, they back down. They don't want to expose their inadequacies.

The boundary less

There are some people who never understand the concept of boundaries. Most people love their personal space and will often put some form of boundaries in certain areas of their life. If its work, they don't bring their private stuff there. If you are such of a person you'll really get frustrated when someone persistently crosses your boundaries. It will be your responsibility to inform such kind of a person of your boundaries and what they can't cross.

You have to mark your boundaries and back them up by your actions. For instance, you can't say you don't want issues of private life in the workplace yet go ahead and engage in small talk regarding other people's issues.

In the workplace, people can often feel overwhelmed by work demands and feel as if some colleagues are making them do their work. The first step to resolving this would be reading and understanding your job description. You'll then be in a good position to say no to something you feel shouldn't be your responsibility. Communicating clearly and making it clear that you understand your role goes a long way in enforcing your boundaries. People will be hesitant to infringe on them. Lastly saying no is something you need to learn. Many people find it difficult to say no to things they feel uncomfortable about, just because you do not want to seem defiant. You then go on to complain later. Practice saying no and meaning it.

The procrastinator

This is one of the most frustrating traits in a workplace. Procrastination normally reflects some form of resistance. This normally happens when a manager wants something done but somebody is not willing to do it and pushes it away each time. That's why there's the concept of deadline and even so, you'll find most people working hard right on the deadline whereas they had time before. This can result in a shoddy job or a failed project. In school, procrastination can also be a bother when in a group; some person keeps on failing to deliver their part on time. At home too, family members will often feel frustrated when something is not done on time by the responsible party. When people keep on procrastinating, they are not interested in the task at hand and will only do it if they have to. Others will procrastinate to prove they hold the power and want others realize that. A boss at work might delay doing something they have to do, especially affecting their staff to show that they hold the power. In such instances, the best way is to avoid getting into a power struggle. If you are the boss, and your staffs are procrastinating on their work, make them understand that they have responsibilities and the role they play in the success of the team. Communicate to them at every stage to find out what challenge they might be facing. In school or at home, people who procrastinate should be made to understand that they are part of a team and their inactions might adversely affect the rest.

The clinging personalities

These are the kind of people who always want to be taken care off. They are insecure on their own and always need a person they perceive stronger than them to guide them. If it's at work, they don't feel confident or qualified enough to handle a task on their own. If it's at home, they can't trust themselves to make a decision. They feel weak and appear desperate. You can't brush these people off since they'll always come back. The best way is to build their confidence. In most cases, they have the ability to handle most tasks but only lack in confidence. Give them responsibility and show them how to handle a situation on their own.

The competitive types

These are the type of people who are always in competition. They perceive every opportunity as a chance to outshine others. They have this utterly competitive attitude that ultimately affects their colleagues. They have a need to always win. When they don't, they feel an injustice has been served. When dealing with these types of personalities, give them an opportunity to win. Let them bask in the glory but then face them with the facts. They are quick to realize when they were wrong and since they have to protect their self-image, they quickly do what's right without creating a fuss.

Victims

These are people who always feel aggrieved and always blame circumstances for whatever situation they find themselves in. They are passive aggressors. Even when it's clear they are wrong, they will somehow find an excuse or blame it on something. When dealing with these kinds of people don't take their victimization. Be firm with them and show them that it's their own fault and nobody has conspired against them.

Complainers

There are chronic complainers who never see anything good. They will complain about anything and everything without offering a solution. These kinds of people are always bitter. They tend to see others as the course of their own angry state without looking inside themselves. When dealing with such kind of people don't agree with what they say. If they start complaining, try making them look for a solution rather than complain.

Chapter 3: Strategies to Manage Difficult Behavior

In this chapter we shall explore different strategies on how to deal with difficult people and get the best from them. Since we can't run away from them, we have to find a way of interacting with them in the best possible way to reduce frustrations on our part. Just as we had seen earlier, people are not normally difficult but under certain circumstances, they might exhibit difficult behavior. We should know of how to deal with this kind of behavior and also tell what situations lead to them and how to avoid them if we can.

The overriding reason people become difficult is due to some form of insecurity or inadequacy. Lack of self-esteem, or social skills might also lead to difficult behavior. A small percentage of people are just aggressive in nature. They will be mean and loud in all situations. However, most difficult people are passive aggressors. They may appear very pleasant and will offer niceties at any opportunity but will also engage in some negative behaviors.

The first strategy when dealing with difficult people is to never take their behavior personally. No matter what they try to do, do not take any offence and focus more on finding a solution rather than dwelling on what they did. Managing our emotions and expectation of people go a long way in reducing frustrations when we encounter aggressive and difficult behavior. When you are dealing with a difficult person never reduce it to personal attacks. Don't become defensive as this might be what their plan is. Stick to the issues at hand and the facts along. Also remember it's not about winning rather than working out how best to relate to each other.

The second strategy is to realize that you can never change someone. This is very critical as some people think that it's possible for a colleague or a partner to change. People never change, they can just pretend for a short time. So the only solution is to understand their behavior and developing strategies to deal with it. The only way a person can change their behavior is through their own personal initiative and this will take some time too. Many managers at work spend a lot of time trying to change an employee to be what they want only to get frustrated when they do not do it. If anybody has to change, then it will only be you. You will need to change your emotional and behavioral responses to difficult personalities. This is by equipping yourself with skills to deal with them.

Dealing with aggressive people

When it comes to aggressive people who might get hostile in their interactions, you'll require to be absolutely clear with them that you do not tolerate their behavior and you will report them to the authorities if they attempt to do something violent. You should interact with them at a neutral place and probably have a third party to keep them in check. If you correspond with them through electronic means, keep a record of the interaction for any future reference. Remember you should never feel threatened somebody's actions. Also don't be angry or otherwise because if so, the other person will have control over you. If you really feel overwhelmed, you'd rather excuse yourself and take some time to regain composure.

Do not judge

It's very tempting to pass judgment on someone based on their behavior. We are quick to label people with some unpleasant names. The bad thing with this is that the person might have been going through a hard time with life's pressures and just reacted in a way that doesn't reflect their true character. Unfortunately, once we label somebody, we will forever view them as that label.

Establish facts

When you encounter a situation, aim first to establish all the facts before you offer a solution. Fast actions are needed from all in today's world, but first establish the facts. Don't allow emotions get in the way of your decision making. You might tend to get angry with a person since they didn't react the way you envisioned, but this shouldn't lead you to making an emotionally charged decision. You might only regret it later. Don't yell or get overly animated. You might be getting worked up on the inside but you must master your self-control. Communication can be through nonverbal means as well, so master your body's language and don't let it give away your emotions. If you allow emotions to get in the way, your team will see you as not being objective. When dealing with difficult people, this would be the last thing you want.

Wait before you react.

When faced with some difficult situations created by a colleague or friend, we tend to react fast in a way that we only regret later. The heat of the moment overcomes us and we say things we shouldn't have said. Whether it's through word of mouth or written communication, we should take some time to let things cool off and approach them with a sober head. At times we don't even need to respond at all. Never lower yourself to mediocrity levels by allowing yourself to respond to negativity. When you fail to respond, you completely disarm the difficult person and alters their pre meditated course of action.

Remove negative people from your life

In certain situations you should remove certain people from your life. Overly negative people who never see anything good will only end up draining you emotionally and inflicting you with their negativity. It will be in your own best interests if you go rid of them. However, if it is not be possible to remove them, for example, if they are colleagues at work or at school and for one reason or another you must work with them, reduce your interactions to the bare necessity. With this, they'll understand your boundaries and will not interfere with them.

Chapter 4: Building a Resilient Mindset

To effectively deal with difficult personalities, you have to develop a resilient mindset. Resilience is the ability to cope with daily life stresses without losing your cool. Resilient individuals are rarely troubled by other people's behavior and as such, they tend to excel. They overcome any challenge they face due to other people being difficult.

Change your script

We sometimes respond the same way to situations we perceive to be difficult even without taking the specific circumstances into consideration. We blindly follow the same script every time. For instance, some people will react to a person who is yelling by yelling back. This is ingrained in them and they know no other way of dealing with this situation. We should change our behavior in the face of difficulty. Our attitude might be fueling a situation from bad to worse. Aim first to understand where this person is coming from and what their real intentions are. Do they want to get a specific reaction from us? Might they be interested in obstructing us and bringing us down? Are they going through a hard time in their life? When we understand a person, we put ourselves in the best position to respond to them in a way that will be beneficial mostly to us but even to them.

Be stress hardy

Stress hardy people have developed a sense of what's important in life and what's not. They spend their time and energy on only what will improve their lives. All other side shows are shoved aside. They have no skills to deal with a negative or difficult person. They understand that difficult situations and difficult people are a part of life and you'll encounter them along the way but they don't dwell on them. They confront them as soon as they can to minimize the impact of such kind of people on their daily activities. When you don't have control over a situation, you let it pass but when you can influence the outcome of another situation, no matter how difficult people you are dealing with may prove to be.

View a situation from the perspective of others

To be resilient, you have to be ready to view issues from a different perspective. You need to be empathizing to other people and try to understand where they are coming from. Most people don't just decide to be difficult, they might not even think of themselves as such. Their mode of understanding of an issue might be different from yours. For instance, people from different cultures might have a completely different perspective on an issue. Understanding means putting yourself in the other person shoes. You should always behave the same way you expect people to behave towards you.

Communication

A single word at the right time can avert a disaster that was about to happen. In dealing with difficult people, you should always strive to communicate effectively. Communication comes in two ways, verbal and nonverbal. Verbal is the most obvious but a lot of communication happens through nonverbal means as well. You need to learn how to decode nonverbal communication. Some people will not say a word to you but they'll still trouble you. This is common in the workplace where a colleague will just be uncooperative and fail to communicate even when you are supposed to be working together. You also need to learn how to pass on information through nonverbal means. Some nonverbal cues include posture, eye movement, facial expressions and use of hands. Listen actively to both the verbal and nonverbal means to get the full reaction. Some common barriers to effective communication are assumption that the message is received and understood, use of a wrong medium, lack of emotions when delivering the message, communication by intimidation, and use of the wrong communication style

Accept others the way they are

If you are to be resilient, you have to understand others and accept them the way they are without expecting them to change. By accepting others, you understand their strengths and weaknesses and how best to respond to them. Accepting someone involves having realistic expectation of their behavior. If you have prior information that you are dealing with a difficult person, you should expect it and be prepared for it.

Adapting to change

Being able to adapt to change is one of the character traits of resilient people. In all spheres of life, change is now occurring at very fast rate and any person especially leaders who are unable or unwilling to adapt to it, find themselves having trouble dealing with different kinds of people. This change brings about new opportunities, more effective ways of carrying out tasks and greater efficiency at the workplace.

Low levels of anxiety

To be resilient in life and in the workplace, you have low levels of anxiety. The human nature wants us to remain where we are used to. We are most comfortable doing things we have been doing as this brings about a sense of security. However, if we remain doing these things, we might be left behind in our fast paced world. Anxiety is the number one reason that holds people back from implementing something new. Anxiety is mostly driven by negative emotions, past unpleasant experiences, or even fear of the unknown.

Chapter 5: How to handle Difficult Topics

We have all experienced situations where we found it difficult to talk about an issue. It might be at home, in school or in the workplace. Sometimes we are unable to talk and let a situation go out of hand. Normally the difficulty in talking is brought by perception of encountering resistance from the people we are talking to. In the workplace, we experience situations where we were unable to offer feedback to another colleague or even to the boss. We are not sure how they will take it. We tolerate a performance problem unable to speak it out. All these situations will lead to perception that you are dealing with difficult people whereas it is us who avoided the difficult communication in the first place.

CC0 Public Domain pixabay.com

Positive communication is a skill we can learn that will enable us handle difficult topics as well as difficult people. We want to communicate in a manner that doesn't raise emotions. We should communicate in such a manner that those we interact with feel the need to maintain a positive interaction with us. In this way we avoid difficult situations. For instance, you want to talk to your child about substance abuse. You fear that they might get difficult and fail to talk to you about it. You need to dissociate your emotions and maintain a positive attitude to get as much from the discussion as possible. Positive communication doesn't mean we have to agree with the other party and what they say. Rather, we build an environment of trust and respect so that we are able to interact positively in the future.

When dealing with a difficult topic you need to:

Being brief

Be brief in your communication with a difficult person. This means you remain on the issue at hand without deviating to other issues not relating to it. Normally when we get angry, people tend to bring up old issues or frustrations into play. For instance we can start recalling when a colleague at work said something bad about us even though you had moved on from it. This only serves to escalate the situation. Keep it as short a possible but getting as much information as possible. Retain your focus throughout your communication. Being brief entails being very specific about what you are talking about. Address specific instances where you want action or explanations given.

Remain positive

Remain positive and choose to look at the wider picture. Even when you are dealing with a very negative person, do not be reduced to their antics such as name calling or accusations. Choose to be the bigger person. Making positive statements and requests makes a lot of difference. Practice marinating positivity in all your conversations. This doesn't mean you are nice and happy all the time, but when you are working with a difficult person, you don't need to escalate the situation by being difficult as well.

Offer to help out

This goes a long way in diluting a situation. You might be offering some minimal help but the fact you offered that help in the first place will make dealing with people a lot easier. Some people become difficult when they feel overwhelmed by work. If you are a boss, this would help them realize that you care for them and no matter the amount of help you offer, they'll feel more relived. If you are dealing with a friend going through a difficult period, offering them help enables them to open up to you and cease being difficult. Even with children, helping them out in small ways makes them feel loved. What bothers them might be a very small issue in your eyes.

Write it down

When you are anticipating to have a difficult talk with someone, it's important to play the conversation that may occur, then write it down. Focus more on your responses so that you can have a good grasp of the best way to respond. When you read through what you have written, you get to have better sense of how this may pan out. It will also enable you to decide when to lay more emphasis on certain words so that your communication hits home.

CC0 Public Domain pixabay.com

Respond decisively

When you deal with difficult people or situations, you need to act decisively. Never bring about doubt in regards to who you are and what you stand for. Be confident and speak with conviction. Work to avert a crisis by dealing with issues as soon as they arise.

People from all walks of life encounter difficult people and difficult situations all the time. It is how you deal with them and how you turn them around to your advantage that determines if you are really a great person. You should also look inside yourself to know if you are a difficult person as well. You might be the cause of the problems you are trying to solve in the first place.

Chapter 6: Easy rules of Dealing with Difficult People

When dealing with difficult people, your reputation is also on the line. What you do or say might affect your good name. Your mental and emotional health may also be affected. Here are some simple rules to keep in mind when you encounter difficult people.

CC0 Public Domain pixabay.com

Think before you act

Before you respond or do anything, give it a thought and try to predict the likely outcome of such a response. In this way, you'll be avoiding unpleasant situations. If you react abruptly without thinking, you may have to deal with the consequences that may arise. You don't want this burden. When you give a well thought our response, either verbally or by your actions you get that other person to think as well.

Keep your cool

In every situation, always keep your cool, no matter how bad the other person reacts; don't let them get to your head. Nobody has the power to control your temper unless you let them. Keeping your cool disarms the other person since they would be looking for a confrontation and also enables you to think through the best course of action. We have seen people lose their cool in a traffic situation and ending up doing something regrettable. Sure there will be some challenging people who'll stretch your patience but never lose your cool.

Don't take it personally

When you encounter a difficult person always keep in mind that what they are expressing on the outside is just a reflection of their inner turmoil. It's not about you at all, it's about them. Someone might be going through a hard time in their life and are bound to get easily get triggered to anger. The best you should do is to understand them and try helping them deal with the issue at hand in a different way. When someone sees you care about them and empathize with them, they are bound to change their attitude towards you.

Search within

In some situations, a person gets difficult as a reaction to your attitude or behavior. So before you blame or judge, first check within to find out if your attitude is right. This is something difficult to do as most people tend to think that they are not the problem. You might have offended someone even unintentionally. If you find out you might be the cause of different attitude you are experiencing from those close to you, make it a point to resolve the issues. When you do this in a timely manner, you avoid any buildup of bitterness and animosity.

Know your goal

In anything we do we have something we want to achieve, even in our conversations. When you understand what your goal is, you rise above all other petty issues that are normally the cause of difficult interactions with others. You won't seek revenge, neither will you wish to cause any harm to another person.

Listen actively

Most of the arguments we have are brought about by lack of listening. If people employed active listening skills, most conflicts would be avoided. Listen with the intention to understand rather than to respond. Misunderstandings fuel conflicts which can make working with people very difficult. Once you have understood what the other person means both by the verbal and nonverbal communication, you are in a good place to give an appropriate response. You don't have to agree with the other person, but understanding them goes a long way into improving relationships.

Conclusion

Life is made up of complex interactions with different people. At home, in school, at the workplace, we are interacting with people all the time. These interactions often don't go as smoothly as we would like. Sometimes we have to deal with some difficult personalities. We can't run away from them since we are somehow tied to them in the circumstance. Dealing with these kinds of people can be stressful. However, we need to equip ourselves with the skill of handling these people since they are everywhere. We can't let them control us and make us miserable.

One important thing to always keep in mind is that very few people are difficult deliberately. They are just making the decisions they feel are the best for them at that particular time. They might not be conscious of the amount of frustration they bring to other people. Do not judge them or let yourself get angry.

Thus we need to learn how to deal with these personalities. They might be challenging and aggravating, but when we learn how to deal with them, we relive ourselves a lot of pressure. The first step in dealing with such kind of people is to understand them first. Most people, who are perceived as difficult, might not even think they are. They might even act very surprised when you tell them that you feel they are. You might also be difficult and not even know it!

Thank you again for purchasing this book! I Hope this book was of value to you. If so, please take the time to review it on Amazon. It would be greatly appreciated.

If this book was of value to you, you may also be interested in <u>other books by Max Smart</u>.

Consider looking up one of the following books:

<u>All books by Max Smart are available on Amazon so go ahead and read some more.</u>

Notes:

Notes:

www.ingramcontent.com/pod-product-compliance
Lightning Source LLC
Chambersburg PA
CBHW070756180526
45168CB00004B/1639